Taut Caesuras

poems by

Pamela Moore Dionne

Finishing Line Press
Georgetown, Kentucky

Taut Caesuras

Copyright © 2021 by Pamela Moore Dionne
ISBN 978-1-64662-515-4 First Edition
All rights reserved under International and Pan-American Copyright Conventions. No part of this book may be reproduced in any manner whatsoever without written permission from the publisher, except in the case of brief quotations embodied in critical articles and reviews.

ACKNOWLEDGMENTS

Slow Teeth was published in *The Northwind Anthology* 2007
Dipsomaniac Sestina was published in *Switched-On Gutenberg* Volume 4, No. 1, Spring/Summer 1999: Not in Your Right Mind
Fraternal Twins was published in *Shenandoah* 48/4 Winter 1998
Mt. Ellinor was published in the *Pitkin Review*, Risk & Revelation, Fall 2017

Publisher: Leah Huete de Maines
Editor: Christen Kincaid
Cover Art: Pamela Moore Dionne
Author Photo: Elizabeth Becker
Cover Design: Elizabeth Maines McCleavy

Order online: www.finishinglinepress.com
also available on amazon.com

Author inquiries and mail orders:
Finishing Line Press
PO Box 1626
Georgetown, Kentucky 40324
USA

Table of Contents

Slow Teeth 1

Apologia 3

A Thorny Crown for the Martyr 4

Dipsomaniac Sestina 8

Perfect 10

Mining 12

Fraternal Twins 13

Artists and Physicians 14

Love and the Central Nervous System 15

Pssst… You Got Any Dopamine? 16

Mercury Rising 18

Mt. Ellinor 20

Slow Teeth

The house was quiet and the world was calm.*
My fingers lay along a bone ridge
softened by rolling folds of blanket
white as the flesh it warmed.

My fingers lay along a bone ridge,
stained by sunlight
white as the flesh warm
under nails rimmed with broken skin.

Stained by sunlight
riding anemic lips, slow teeth
bite nails rimmed with broken skin,
their path ceaseless as the plow at spring turning.

Anemic lips ride slow teeth,
the metallic taste
ceaseless as the plow at spring turning.
A flow of platelets through arteries,

the metallic taste
like blood at the cuticle's heart.
An errant flow of platelets through arteries
begins to bump and patter against nightfall.

Like blood at the cuticle heart,
a blue anaerobic god-pulse
bumps, patters against night.
Taut caesuras, breath as punctuation.

A blue god's anaerobic pulse,
narrow as the moon cutting through glass,
breathes punctuation to taut caesuras.
All linear equations falter.

A narrow moon cuts through the window
into rolling folds of blanket.
All linear equations falter.
The house is quiet, the world calm.

from Wallace Stevens' poem

APOLOGIA
For my brother, August 25, 1998

One year after your suicide you visit me anew. Nightly.
This time there is no bloody visage, only you nightly.

Yours is the light I saw once long ago after a car wreck left me
following the warmth, bathing in its brilliant hue nightly.

For days I stood outside my body, wanting in and wanting out.
I chased the flow of my ambivalence through and through, nightly.

I know where you are. I've seen the colors of that corona. It's us,
the universe's constant energy. You're not alone. It's not just you nightly.

Forgive my anger. I missed your voice calling *Sammy Lee*,
routing those lost dreams that visit the indigo blue, nightly.

A Thorny Crown for the Martyr
For Willis Earl Moore, Jr.

The arterial circle of Willis
resides at the base of the brain.
Substance flows through circuitry like train
terminals or the vines on a trellis.
The pia mater sips her wine, instills us
with the nourishment of gray matter reined
like a cultivated stallion's bobbed mane,
through very narrow anastomoses.

What coincidence led me to this view
of blood and bone and main cerebral arteries?
Why have you, in life, haunted me like this?
In death you haunt me still. What is it you do?
What is this clank and rattle, this phlegmy wheeze?
I tire of all this vinegar and piss.
***

I tire. This is all vinegar and piss.
My fingerprints don't mark the thirty-eight
that took your life. Let's get that straight.
You took a shot impossible to miss.
All those IQ points and you gave us this?
I'm angry. I felt your urned weight,
bore it full in my arms, walked through a gate,
scattered your ashes to feed the fish.

Brother, your guilty daughter forgives—
you, not herself. You now walk saintly ground.
She crashes through the accidental days you left her.
Your son cried when the ashes spread in drifts,
vermiculite sinking under a pthalo green Puget Sound.
He spoke about your military service, a heartfelt detour.
***

He spoke of military service, his heartfelt detour
for the feelings he possessed. He refused
the heft of human ash, his fingers unused
to sorrow, unwilling to tackle the pour.
This is your legacy. This is what you
bent your purpose to. Your total fused.
Condensed to cinder and regret. So abused.
Your children's childrens' view of you a blur.

Now that they won't know a living man
as grandfather, they turn to cousins, uncles—
any testosterone marriages provide.
For the rest of time, we see you as drifting sand.
These are the things we work out, the wrinkles.
Capacity varies. Some gaps are too wide.

***

Capacity varies. The gaps are wide.
We have never understood
what drove you into densely aching moods.
Your navy discharge described another side,
the magnetic opposites you denied.
You called it an act played for the good
of your fellow inmates—and you—who would
benefit from life on a civilian ride.

They said you were mentally unstable.
You said all you wanted was out.
Now we know the sty that mired you. I'm sorry
I helped you create an indelible
charade behind a chilled glass of stout.
They're all the same, these addict stories.

***

They're all the same, these addict stories.
Somebody's brother, sister, mother, son,
a father. I could have been the one
to carry on tradition. Injuries
like this come in genetic codes, slurries
we can't escape. No one yet has won
freedom under the inherited thumb.
Every corpse dies of some small worry.

Alcoholism is Willis the Elder's gift
to junior. Buy the house a round, full circle.
Welcome home your sons and daughters.
In my own child I pray for a rift
in a march delivered through the cervical.
Think genetics and cannon fodder.
***

I think genetics and cannon fodder
each time any one of us gets too drunk,
too stoned, or starts to look like father
on Saturday afternoons when he stunk
of cigarettes and alcohol and drunk
booze sloshed into a glass, no water.
As kids, we sat in bars while Dad debunked
all the psychological theories of bothered

children worried about what's next.
Though kids wonder, they also simply trust.
You were that trusting child once but got lost
in the crazy quilt of DNA and biological text.
One mother dumped you, followed her own thrust.
To that dura mater you were dross.
***

To that hard mother you were less than dross.
Did she sell you or just give you away?
I never knew. Your father's only boy,
he didn't find you; not till rickets bossed
your spine and a new wife replaced his loss.
You were old enough by then to be swayed
by anger and distrust; the world too splayed
for one so young, so clumsily tossed.

I loved you. More than that—I adored.
When did the words stop? The *I love you's*
between us? When did empty mouths start to kill us?
Brother, where are you now? Some nether shore?
My blood continues round, feeds my brain through
the arterial circle of Willis.

Dipsomaniac Sestina

For years you replenished dopamine to lush levels
in tropical synaptic zones, flooded riotous limbic rivers
with Jack Daniels. The dendritic pathways of the flow
deltaed on a corpus callosum so awash in the sediment
of acetylcholine that a white hemispheric substance,
once cerebral, grew base, grew stupid, grew profane.

Behind every point bar lies a levee. Deeper in lie profane
swampy syndromes and manias dependent on chemical levels,
driven by genetic hierarchies that lead to substance
abuse. Choose your poison; its availability measured in rivers,
if you know where to look. Beware the muddy sediment.
Swim only within the bars where you find a clear flow.

Had we scanned the corpus callosum, evidenced a flow
of hypometabolic distress; your PET jealously profane.
We might not have called you a drunk had we seen the sediment,
this disorder larger than addiction, had we recognized the levels
that propelled you, diving head first, into murky gator riddled rivers.
If we are guilty at all, it's for this simple lack of substance.

But you? You found substance where there was no substance.
You panned the gaps and eddies of the raphe nuclei's flow
for golden serotonin nuggets. You built dopamine damned rivers.
In our mouths your name tumbled, a lost tooth bloody and profane.
Your intellect failed. You sunk to weighted levels,
just so much suspended erratic against the sediment

of our lives. You became the boozy sediment
present at holiday gatherings; a stinking substance
tracked in on someone's soul, no one daring to level
a complaint regarding the odorous flow.
You brokered the thing we denied. You were profane
in your adoration of besotted rivers.

You were our Stanley hunting Livingston, finding the source of rivers
where you were caught in Victoria's plunge pool sediment,
tangled in the meander of a floodplain so profane
you couldn't find your way out, couldn't find the substance
of the self that would track into safer flows.
Finally, there were only so many levels

below sea level you were willing to travel, only so many rivers'
muddy flows you would swim, abraded by coarse sediment.
Some dives profane the sport, yours gave it substance.

Perfect

Arthrogryposis Multiplex Congenita: a term describing the presence of multiple joint contractures at birth. It is relatively rare, occurring in perhaps 1 in 3,000 births. —AVENUES support group pamphlet

Wet lung is the least of your problems.
I watch your labored breathing,
a plastic tube taped to the curve
of your nose. My breath quickens,
pacing with yours. Skin soft and pink
as the underside of my wrist,
hair a brown blur of spider web.

I lift the receiving blanket,
my retinas acid-etched with weeping.
Your feet
> round as rubber balls,
> absolute orbs
> except for ten toes
> with silk nails.

They press against your shins
at an almost exact 180° from the ankle.
Your legs are stiff, unjointed at the hip.
They are bowed to an O
like the *Ohs* we made
when our son said
something's wrong.
He disappeared,
leaving us with that terrible unknowing
our hungry mouths
oval as the *Oh* given in solace
by friends who take us in their arms
and rock us the way we rock you.
Both your femurs fractured at birth
> common, they say, with this disease.

We wait. The *Ohs* soften
as we hold you against our bodies.

A legion of doctors march through the ICU
        neurosurgeons, geneticists, orthopedic surgeons.
They tell us of caudal dimples, domed fontanelles,
dislocated hips and pulmonary hypertension.
Fortune tellers all, parsing the unreadable signs.
Days pass. Each of us breathes the now
that we are given.

Mining

The whine, high pitched,
spinning through sterile air,
acrid burnt bone.
Dust coats my tongue.
In Victorian England a mark of beauty
was a full set of teeth.
Even nearly full would do.

I'm a post war child dragged around America,
raised on unfluoridated well water.
My cavernous mouth is filled with amalgams
flawed by acid rains of tea, coffee, Pepsi,
and face-first contact with unyielding terra firma.
I used to set off metal detectors at airports.
Now I'm mostly porcelain with gold-bearing punctuations.
And still I sit in my dentist's chair.
His gloved hands wield a stainless pick,
a miner's light looms from his forehead.

Ampoule after ampoule
2% lidocaine, 3% mepivacaine—
my lip the size of our front porch.
I cannot help but think at times like this
of days when whiskey was the only novocain.
Barbers carried shot glasses and pliers,
sent bloody drunks reeling from itinerant clinics,
brass spittoons laced with more than chaw.

Fraternal Twins

Crow and I, we spread our wings together,
long narrow bones of ulna and radius nearly identical.
Except for density, I could fly away.
We are fraternal twins born of the same nature.

The long narrow bones of ulna and radius nearly identical.
A blue heron hunts shallows, metatarsals wet to the ankle.
We are fraternal twins born of the same nature.
I gird myself in neoprene to the hips and match stance.

A blue heron hunts shallows, metatarsals wet to the ankle.
Her flesh covers a cranium protecting a fragile brain.
I gird myself in neoprene to the hips and match stance.
Waves lap against her, green-gray. Crow circles overhead.

The heron's flesh covers a cranium, protects a fragile brain.
My cerebrum is likewise encased inside a skull.
Waves lap against us, green-gray. Crow circles overhead.
Like her, I search. Within us all the same imperative.

My cerebrum is likewise encased inside a skull.
Except for density, I could fly away.
Like these birds, I search. It's the same imperative.
Crow and I, we spread our wings together.

Artists and Physicians

I.

Two disciplines study the anatomy of human form.
Medicine views musculature laid over bone as concrete system.

Artists view anatomy from a gestural stance.
Each discipline peels away layers to reveal truth.

Artists peel only a figurative skin. Their anatomy is metaphor.
A physician removes layer after layer to reach what is beneath.

At one time it was hard to tell art student from medical student.
Both involved themselves in the workings of cadavers.

II.

My first experience with a human skeleton was in life drawing class.
These bones belonged to a once healthy young man.

What was left of him came from Cambodia in the seventies.
I could not sketch this remaindered human with anything but anguish.

A sudden familiarity with the unknown dead can render uneasy alliances.
I pictured a student, or perhaps a teacher like me, perhaps with a family.

In his country, intellectuals were marked for slaughter and mass graves.
Here, a long dead anatomy professor continues his career.

Love and The Central Nervous System

The main part of the central nervous system
Is found within the skull.
It's a mass of pinkish gray nerve cells.
Approximately ten billion all in all.

Found within the skull
are glial cells, blood vessels, even secretory organs.
Approximately ten billion, all in all.
It's a complex, a triumvirate.

Are glial cells, blood vessels, even secretory organs
what drive us into serotonin highs and lows and in betweens?
It's a complex, a triumvirate,
a massive stroke of genius.

What drives us into serotonin highs and lows and in betweens?
Love is just like that
a massive stroke of genius
driving toward oblivion.

Love is just like that.
It's a mass of pinkish gray nerve cells
driving toward oblivion.
The brain is that part of the central nervous system.

PSSST… YOU GOT ANY DOPAMINE?

In the nucleus acumbens resides
a rich deposit of basal dendrites,
a gold mine of neurotransmitters.
Among these is dopamine
nature's own Pavlovian bell.
We are addicted to its rush.

Wrap your arms around me and I get a rush.
That's why all along with lust resides
this drive, this tolling of the bell
that makes us drool. Our dendrites
begin the Macarena to a dopamine
orchestra of chemical transmitters.

Then we become the transmitters,
the bearers of a genetic rush
to copulate until we zone on dopamine
to keep filling those quotas of new resides,
the birth of which guarantee fresh pools of dendrites
to keep us going into infinity, drooling, ringing the bell.

I'm not sure nature meant to keep the bell
clanging away, sending out those transmitters
of pleasure, dancing with those dendrites
at quite the levels that we do. Though fools rush
in and that appears to be where man resides,
man is not a complete idiot, a dope. I mean…

Really! Let's get this addiction to dopamine
under control. Enough! Stop ringing the damn bell.
The fate of this planet is at stake—resides—
in our ability to figure new ways to be transmitters.
Can we survive our instinct for pleasure? Halt the rush?
Does pleasure without progeny mean unhappy dendrites?

Not necessarily. Stimulate those dendrites
but use a condom. Keep general dopamine
levels constant without the population rush.
For all I care, you can ring and ring and ring your bell.
Just remember, if you transmute zygotes, you transmit heirs.
This is the pivot point on which everything resides.

Pleasure resides in branching dendrites
flooded by transmitters washed with dopamine.
Inside the cranial bell, an easy, natural, addict's rush.

Mercury Rising

Fifteen years old in the back seat
of my mother's 1960 Mercury Monterey.
Mom driving, Aunt Dottie beside her talking,
my 4-year-old cousin sitting between
me and my older sister on that broad back bench.
Traffic is tight on this day before Thanksgiving.
I died that day. Went through the windshield.
No seatbelts back then.

The woman who crossed the centerline
was eating a sandwich and drinking coffee
on her way to work the night shift
at the Bremerton Naval Yard. They said
she must have tried to hit her brake
but got the gas pedal instead.
By the time she plowed into us
head-on
she was doing eighty.
It totaled the Mercury.
She died that day, too.
Hers stuck, mine didn't.

We met in the emergency room
looking down on ourselves
from far above
those bloody bodies.
Neither one of us felt pain.
I was calm, she terrified.
I knew her concerns for her children,
a husband who didn't seem like much.
She had to take the walk so I went along.

That light is real. Octarine[1].
Every color you know plus a lot you don't.
When you walk into the glow, it's warm
and filled with singing. Beautiful voices
in a tongue we've forgotten.
I felt wrapped in glory,
didn't want to go home
though I knew I would.

[1]*Octarine, a color created by Terry Pratchett in the Discworld series.*

Mt. Ellinor

gravity screams lion-voiced
on the west side   I'm trapped
a tight glissade run
worn deep by other climbers
ice razors   blue-white blur
slope rushes upward against thighs   buttocks
below me a rock stack
        huge   unyielding
stone cold air   urine scent of mountain goat
blood salt taste   sharp teeth clashing
        against tongue

    sound   a desperate creature
caught in the cavern of my mouth
its arc fighting a larynx
taut with adrenalin

tethered to my skittering axe
useless trail of ballast   I feint
parry   the blade batters
my arm   my head   my shoulder
    a blind assault

the rock stack rises to meet me
    you stand before it
    two hundred feet
if we make contact I'll take you with me

I hear hard pack ice hammering
    more than I feel it
my heels stutter   stumbling
scrabbling   I dig in
    brace   flex my knees
the slope slows its onrush   I dig in harder
    harder   regain the axe
    the mountain ceases to move

nothing to it   my hands shake   my knees quiver
I can't stand up   so I plant my axe a little too firmly
begin more carefully   by the time I reach you
        I've considered
        what I've done to save myself

Poet, writer and visual artist, **Pamela Moore Dionne**'s first chapbook, *Paradox and Illusion*, was published by Finishing Line Press in September 2020. Her work has appeared in a number of journals, magazines and online publications including *Shenandoah, Pontoon, Crab Creek Review, Switched-on-Gutenberg* and *Snow Monkey*. Dionne was a Seattle, Washington Jack Straw writer and received their Artist Support Grant to record a CD of her Sabina Spielrein Ghazal series. The CD was recorded with composer Jim Knodle and pianist/composer Lynette Westendorf's musical accompaniment. Dionne earned a Centrum Foundation residency for her series of classical form poems re-animating the cadaver terminology of Gray's Anatomy. She earned a Washington State Artist Trust Gap Grant for work on a narrative piece of fiction about an elderly interracial couple. She has had nonfiction published in magazines and journals including **Raven Chronicles** and *Pacific Northwest Writers Association's Author Magazine*. Her visual art has been published in journals and magazines as well as being presented in one-woman shows in the Seattle area. Other credits include founding and managing the online art and literature journal *Literary Salt*. Dionne received her MFA from Goddard College and lives in Port Townsend, Washington with her husband Ron and a vizsla puppy named Magda.